Yoga/ii
Poems Along the Way

Poems Along the Way

A. Tapasiddha

Copyright © 2023 A. Tapasiddha (Nitya Dambiec)

All rights reserved. Alimentanima Books.

ISBN: 978-0-6455649-2-1

From the Editors

This collection of poems was originally published in 2019 until the title *Intangible Things Set Free*. Due to its interest not only as a collection of poems, but also as a book of insights into the yogic path as a spiritual search, we have decided to republish it with a new title and cover, so as to make it available to those interested in this side of the book, as well as the poetic one.

When written, the author, originally from New Zealand, was working as a yogic nun, and had taught and travelled in Asia, Europe, and South America in this capacity. She had chosen this path aged eighteen and had been living in this way for around fifteen years at the time. These poems, along with their literary value, serve as a record of her reflections and experiences during this period. They also serve, therefore, as a useful point of reflection for others practising yoga and meditation, or for those interested in the search for self-awareness and the processes and development of human consciousness and emotions in general.

We have included the original prologue, as we believe it will also be of interest to many readers.

Prologue
(From the first edition)

Life itself is intangible. It is like love, happiness, the soul, passion and emotion, and so many other such ideas that we think we can hold onto in order to sustain us but which, ephemeral, escape between our fingers the more we desire to fasten them to ourselves. We feel the need to ensure a continuous flow of sensations in order to compensate for other feelings which abruptly shake us, until we become accustomed to having them close by, although still lacking the capacity to properly discern how to control them.

In the same way that science speaks of dark matter and energy, whose origin and nature are unknown to us but whose presence we are aware of (albeit indirectly), what we call the 'inner life' arouses the suspicion that there is something inside us which moves according to its own criteria, not entirely accessible to our knowledge or command. What some interpret as simple electro-chemical reactions of substances circulating in a supposedly – up to a certain point – autonomous organ called the brain, others consider as an undoubtable link not only with our physical surroundings, the body, and the socio-cultural and environmental conditions that encircle us, but also with other 'in-stances' that indirectly hint of their existence.

Contra to the desire to make increasingly tangible things which in fact are not, with the hope of being able to retain and make permanent those concepts which 'go together with life' (identity, status, family, nationality, etc.), there are currents of thought which, coming from diverse ideological positions, attempt to offer a less 'solid' expression of life. Through art, philosophy, or religion, there are suggested other 'less limiting' options, if they must be described in some way, although in these cases we also, all to often, end up resorting to models that enclose our ideas within certain defined spaces, aiming to differentiate themselves by marking out territories through which the entry of certain groups of people and not others is allowed, and we therefore fall back upon the same narrowness which we wanted to avoid.

In the concerned text, the author, A. Tapasiddha, opens up for us a perspective that unites the Eastern spiritual tradition with the world of forms and processes which we identity as 'nature', and through the projection of deep emotion, ensconces us in a unique 'mind-body-spirit' realm, the final goal of all unifying tendencies that search for an integrated theory explaining the existence of life in particular and the universe as we understand it (so far).

From the very first verse, we are offered the possibility of redemption. Everything flows, everything changes, life is an ethereal landscape upon which one will encounter distinct moments which help to forward our evolution, through the mental turbulence that promises to free us from (our own) darkness. It is this continuous transformation which whispers to us of ancient wisdom: that the permanent lies within the process. The opposite, the apparent contradiction to this, is the seed of stillness, of that so longed for calm, which, paradoxically, is born from the whirlwind. Sadness and discouragement appear to us full of charm. Like a joking trickster who actually assails us with benevolence in disguise, regret is the key to joy, and only a thin line separates grief from ecstasy: in the pendulum's desire for rest, peace and euphoria struggle, unaware that they are twin sisters.

And here we enter, as sentient beings trying to decide if the force of will is truly our own, or something foreign to us. We have the horizon in our hands, the sun between our fingers, and yet, sometimes we are still unable to perceive that what we want is closer than we think, or rather, that it is even prior to the discourse, already within us. And also outside us, completing the 'univer-somatic' entity that we strive to divide. What A. Tapasiddha is proposing to us is to fearlessly climb the first steps of a stairway towards the inner sky, to stop dragging the ego which weighs us down and which we do not want to let go of due to the fear aroused by the existential vacuum which entails creating distance with an identity which, on the other hand, we have not constructed alone. Jumping, let's plunge into the endorphic river, whose circular current of storm and tranquillity always carries us to the ocean of which we are a part.

The author reminds us that each 'I' carries a mixed halo, that we are a flower born of various seeds, and in this mix resides a fragrance that is unique yet universal. It is like the moon of our dreams, hiding a face that we will never be able to love if we do not imagine it as if like the landscape that captivates us. Intertwined with the external world, there is another beauty which we do not see, or which we do allow ourselves to see as our own. One should live with thirst! Let us challenge ourselves, taste life from all angles, as heirs of all cultures, children and grandchildren of every race and condition. We are transient beings building bridges between scattered souls, but each time we try to complete the circle of unity, the system blocks us, and with disastrous consequences for both those who are outside as well as those inside, who will remain with their thirst to humanity unquenched.

We all breathe the same air, are formed by the same water. We are the container and also its contents, but above all, we are the membrane which separates these, and which is subject to all variety of manifestations. We are ever permeated by the light which comes and goes, whose origin and destiny we are incapable of clearly defining; we are drifting ships which find their route upon each change of the wind, each variation of the current. Like the clay from which the container is formed, our nature crosses the line between the inanimate and the living, leaving us no clear clues to discern where the exact limit lies. Those who have tried have, too often, run into the 'Cruelty of Real Life', losing contact with the source from which the essence of consciousness flows, which is like an exquisite nectar that must be sipped very slowly. That is to say, we stuff ourselves full with dense, viscous syrup which entraps and consumes us, and stubbornly believe that this is the natural environment that we require in order to be able to claim that we have enjoyed the fruits of our troubled passage through the world. We even end up convincing ourselves that this is a redeeming mission, when in reality we have not even been able to face up to our own salvation.

Here lies the grand task that A. Tapasiddha proposes to us: to take on the great adventure that leads to the limits of our 'planet-I', and to the discovery of the universe concentrated within each human being; a journey without luggage but with the willingness to cross territories where, without warning, we will find trunks full of memories that we have left behind, from journeys already done, but without having paused to watch the view. From the horizon upon the river, castles of stars, the earth trembling under rain-showers, the sea's sad currents, the breath of mountains, bridges of dreams, or waterfalls of flowers in the decrepit gardens of wealthy neighbourhoods, all these roads are made familiar to us: they are the desired transit towards places which we have been otherwise replacing with a 'show of life', with an anxiety to conquer new experiences, more external than eternal, and that deceive us with their seductive challenge. We have to reach the peak! We must conquer discouragement, surpass ourselves! When everything in the world is calling us towards an apparently obligatory challenge of domination of the visible, be it in the form of emotions or excursions, A. Tapasiddha, to the contrary, tells us that the stormy chasms are also essential destinations, and will carry us towards the supposedly unattainable core of the universal soul.

The inner path, however, is not decorated only with flower petals. In our loneliness as solitary travellers, only our own heartbeats will leave a mark, we will meet in the darkness of night, and then separate, always with the hope of meeting again. Love is a path that does not permit short-cuts nor retreat. We will all meet there sometime, pilgrims of our souls, as part of a common heart which should be unwrapped without hurry or fear. This collective existence, this immense tapestry woven of smiles and tears which extinguish some fires whilst enlivening others, is what makes the seemingly impossible obtainable: unconditional love is one of the central milestones to crown our continuous ascent. The challenge requires courage, there is nothing to grab onto as you climb, no map to guide one: life is like that, open, intangible, one flame freed from another fire that has already been extinguished.

Like acrobats on a tightrope, we set our limits without realising that it is we ourselves who have created all the paraphernalia that we need to 'feel alive.' We fear the great author and director of the drama in which we act. Let us rid ourselves of all our clothing and run free, decorated only with garlands of victory, and flowingly surrender to the world, with our only doubt being into which expression of the infinite we will enter, directed by the unknown, in intimate ecstasy. To fall in love with intangible love, and to release the same into the hands of our fellow travellers, to their pleasure or even not, to these adventures the author invites us: to explore such unfathomable places, carrying the best tools available to us, until we appear (or disappear) as our true selves.

Francisco Guerra
January 15, 2019.

POEMS

-1-

Today the flower of my mind
has swirling grey-cloud petals,
like black ink dancing on a wet page.

Amidst those restless petals
I find poems;
amidst the brewing of a storm,
tranquillity;
amidst the humid pressure,
the contradictory mingling
of turbulence and calm,
I wait
for the release of rain,
for freedom.

the promise of change
composes songs upon my heart,
and my grey storm-cloud flower murmurs,
as if about to open.

-2-

The walls of my palace
are built from the living cells of plants,
creeping, climbing, blooming,
ever transforming.
My kingdom is a garden,
its gates two giant trees,
and beyond them,
an array of gods and goddesses
waiting to be worshipped in the form of flowers,
buzzing bees humming their hymns of adoration,
each entity returning the worship of the other,
the sun smiling back on the dew-drop shoots of plants,
bees drunk
after finding their altars filled with honey.

In my palace there are no marble arches
imbued with a history of despotism,
disguised behind an artistry of servitude:
my worship is of a bud that blooms, dies,
and scatters its seeds,
of the unrehearsed dance of riverside-reeds in the breeze,
of the attraction of rain to the earth
and a pomegranate tree to the sun,
of the incredible orange of pomegranate petals
scattered on green grass,
and the iridescence of a dragonfly
drinking raindrops as they run along
the round bodies of unripe fruits,
finally falling from their star-shaped crowns.

At the altar of my pomegranate tree
I worship the song of infinity
that whispers through notes of transience,
and the mastery of resilience and grace
that combines in the arched branches dangling
with spheres filled with blood-red seeds.

Marble arches are long-lasting but not eternal.
Life however, is fleeting, yet has no end:
blossoms fall, fruits form,
seeds give birth and die over and over.
Once you have seen all of a marble castle,
that is really all of it,
but my garden
is an artwork of constant transformation.
Try to know it totally,
and you will become absorbed in it,
surrendering, confounded.

With every flower as an altar,
and ever day the altars newly-born,
the walls of my palace
are the living cells of greenery.
No cell of it desires the permanence of stone,
yet every one is yearning for eternity.
I own not this palace,
and rule over no one:
it reigns over and teaches me,
touching through impermanence
the edges of infinity.

-3-

Sadness too has her enchantment,
which does not yet incline me
to cast her utterly aside.

A cloaked figure in the night,
hunched over the river's shadowed banks,
muttering some bewitchment,
intermingled with the susurration of the water
as all around are slumbering,
she is not as malicious as she seems.

Her dark back stooped
over the sombre waters
hides a million things.
I know she is a trickster,
her intentions residing in the twilight,
and in the night-blooming flowers
that cry at dawn.
She is inclined to dwell in abandoned hamlets
and ill-aligned junctures of time,
in all places not so easily defined.

It is not the first time
we have stumbled upon one another,
here by the new moon river,
and I know that any moment
she might turn,
night's shadowed shawl falling
to deliver a shimmering waterfall of black hair
and the most impossibly joyous
of guileless smiles.

In her uncovered hands she proffers
a mug moulded from red river clay,
an offering of the stream's singing waters,
gurgling and murmuring,
sunlight laughing around its rims,
enveloped still by the sounds of night all around.

Her cloak of malevolence
is all to often a benevolent guise,
and so I shall not ask her yet be banished.

-4-

Don't you know
that sadness,
pure sadness,
is also a beautiful creature?

Better any day
that a basketful of superficial smiles
and the cynic's search for happiness
in pretence.

The question of beauty
lies in its integrity,
in the purity of your grief:
feel it, a moment,
you are human after all.

Don't you know
that pain is one of the keys
to the door of joy?
That the difference between sorrow and ecstasy
is so very small?
I promise you,
I promise even the cynical crowd of the world,
that joy is real,
and it is a joy so pure
that when you unlock its door,
words fall silent,
and only tears shall fall.

-5-

If sorrow be a compulsion towards elation
and inadequacy to perfection,
then let my joy be so pure
that it reaps no persuasion
to swing back into pain.

Contrary to the convictions of the world
the pendulum does not really seek
to oscillate endlessly,
left to right, loss to gain,
for eternity.
It rather has in sight another,
gravity-defying, centre:
peace,
where it wishes to remain.

This peace is my euphoria,
ecstasy which wills no antonym,
so pure that it fulfils itself
and triumphs over everything in this imperfect world.

-6-

What are you gazing at, longingly,
in the distance,
as you sit after bathing,
contemplating your existence
upon the morning-sun warmed river stone?
With which promises did the horizon captivate you,
as you poured streams of water,
glittering and gleaming,
over your body,
water filled with the
murmuring sing-song sounds
of the river caressing angled rocks and rounded stones?

For which fulfilment does your heart aspire
upon the intangible horizon,
so far away?

Run your hands
through the sun-warmed water a moment,
rivulets caressing your palms,
sunbeams twirling around your fingertips.
What you long for in the distance
is just there, swirling between your fingers.

And look!
There it is again in the dance of sunlight
slipping in and out between your toes!
The same sun you search for out upon the skyline
is reflected right there
in the drops falling from your hair,
sliding down your spine.

And look!
Now they are caught on your eyelashes,
and have fallen into your eyes.
You need not stretch your gaze so far away
to find what your heart is seeking.

-7-

Finally
we are alone again,
just You, I,
and silence.
As the dawn greets the sky
its reflection
ascends inside me,
a refreshing breeze around me,
and again the same within.
The earth and I were both hoping
for the coolness of this moist morning,
and after so many days of rainless waiting
we are ready to receive
every drop of dew.
The sun rises,
the leaves of plants drink thirstily,
the universe moves around me,
and everything duplicates itself
again anew within me.

-8-

I stand in front of a step,
one more upon an inner stairway
that ever calls me.
It is a step towards the irresistible unknown,
yet something within me continues to resist.
It is a step towards a friend so familiar
that sometimes we avoid embracing
for fear of merging,
yet it is for that very purpose that we meet.
To take that step
I must let go of something:
to become my Self,
I must cast aside
another layer of myself,
loosing forever my footing
on the stairway that falls behind me.
I know that I will take it:
the fearfully exhilarating question
is whether I should take it now,
or will I withdraw again and wait?

-9-

What a strange river this is,
twisting and turning
in wayward ways,
only to terminate, finally,
back at its source.

What a singularly strange river this is,
rushing in full circle,
around again to where it started.

What strange waterfalls
there are to be found upon its rocky rapids,
simultaneously cascading cool sweetness upon me,
and rising in an upward rush within.

My boat has flown upon its gushing waters,
paused in its stagnant curves,
floated in quiet pools filled with night's fallen stars,
and relished its waterfalls.

I have quenched my throat
with its strange water
which always left me thirstier
and my body has lain
immersed within its enticing currents,
almost dissolving,
but finally always reappearing.

What a strange river this is,
that has carried me so far,
and now, with its end in sight,

leaves me listening
to softly lapping water
that whispers, 'don't rush, wait just a little…'

I had forgotten my origin,
and now here I am again.
My boat is the same,
only a little more rugged,
but when I gaze into the river,
it is clear,
there is no face reflecting back at me,
only placid water,
perfectly still.

-10-

Waves, frothing,
thrash against each other,
as if determined
to drown one another.
One submerges the other,
and then each surfaces again
and so goes on the cycle
of their endless game.

Above the waves,
wind whirls,
battling against itself,
the army of one side
continuously merging into the other.

Watching
one would think the waves are fighting,
so too the wind,
but they are one body,
dancing with itself,
their friction a façade,
as the watery breakers shatter
the reflected moon to pieces
and then discover it again,
its intensity renewed.

The stormy winds of joy,
ecstatic in festivity,
waltz with sorrowful sensibilities,
around and round,
as the waves and wind also intermingle.

But the waves are not the ocean,
and the wind is not the sky,
though as they dance,
diving in and out of infinity,
they deceive us that they are,
and we believe them,

until,
for a moment,
they are calm,
and the sea is just the sea,
an unruffled continuity,
and the sky, un-flurried,
reveals itself,
allowing the moon,
for a moment,
to shine still and unbroken.

-11-

You have asked me about my lineage,
and I would like to reply that the scattered seeds
of red-flowering coral trees
were my womb,
their brilliant crimson spring candles of flowers
adorning leafless tree-tops my noble name-sake:
at once majestic and unpretentious, that would be perfect.
Perhaps for show I could also claim
some royal strains of orchid as my ancestors,
though I must admit
that my inheritance probably contains
a greater percentage of dandelion seeds,
sprouting accidentally in the pavement,
trodden on and broken.

My lineage rests in the smile of a girl
in love with butterflies,
and of a boy who saves moths from street-lamps.
There is also a portion derived
from a body misused and abandoned,
from the cold stares of uncaring strangers,
and words of abuse towards an outcast:
no one is a child only of innocence.

My ancestral line most likely includes
the smell of boiled cabbages and turnip leaves
in an equal or greater degree
to silver-leafed halva sprinkled with rose-water.

The history of my parentage includes rivers
which consummated their love with mountains.

I hope that the mountains were green
and the river water pure,
though I expect that it was tainted somewhat
by the soap of bathing pilgrims,
scattered with the litter of lazy travellers.

The smoke of sandalwood incense
smothers the scent of sewerage in street gutters,
and sometimes vice-verse.
These are also truths,
but they do not make the evening breeze less perfect.

If my lineage contains kings,
then I hope it also contains some toilet-cleaners
and garbage-collectors
to add a smattering of humility to the scales of arrogance.

There are fingers writing poems,
hands tending the earth in the vegetable garden,
calloused hands stacking bricks,
and tender hands on violin strings
crying the songs of a brick-makers longings,
which have endured thirsty days of hot sun and hunger,
yet still believe in God.

I hope that there is a saint somewhere in my ancestry,
though he probably started as a sinner.

The branches of my family tree make for a twisted and confounding story:
they contain poverty and riches,
though you may mistake one for the other;
there are fighters who are peaceful,

and pacifists who cannot sleep at night;
wise fools,
and foolish wisdom.

I have five kinds of jasmine in my garden,
from five corners of the world,
and in the evening breeze they all mingle,
indistinguishable.
My lineage is like that:
attempting to tear apart the pieces of its aroma
could be tedious.
I will not stop you trying,
but don't mind if I chuckle at your attempts.
Just breathe the scent of all the jasmines mixed together,
it is better,
especially when the dandelions in the lawn decide to join,
unknown and uninvited.

-12-

I dream of the moon,
and in my dreams
she is always full,

but when my eyes open,
she is sometimes waxing,
sometimes waning,
and I must seek her at times in darkness,
other-times in light.

Awake at night,
maybe I will delight in her manifested form,
maybe I will discover her formless embrace,
or maybe I will find her,
dancing elusively between both these spaces,

but in my dreams,
when I close my eyes,
she is my beloved,
and she is always full.

-13-

This cascading of flowers upon me
from the treetops,
a blushing carpet showered
upon the canopy floor,
are they only petals,
or does their enchantment lie elsewhere?

Are they only plant-cells
composed in an appealing symmetry,
or is this cascade also an inner one,
flowing inside me,
vibrations from the treetops of my soul
blooming upon the branches of my mind,
and falling as the quivering joy
of my feet's dancing caress
upon the earth?

This anointment with blossoms,
is its beauty only in its tangible presence?
Or is it in its whispers
of something else,
in the eternally intermingling flow
of internal and external worlds?

-14-

Leaf, uncurling
your fresh-formed tip unfurling,
who calls you?
What destiny draws you
to open, unfolding?
What irresistible pull
has caused you
to reach out seeking
strange worlds beyond worlds,
where mystery shifts into reality,
reality into mystery,
abodes where words,
inarticulate, fall,
where far and near converge,
known and unknown merge.

What are you trying to touch,
tender-sprouting leaf-tip?
Oblivious to everything,
to where are you reaching,
as the dawn-light-sipping dewdrops
slip-slide, gliding,
off your exuberantly quivering body
that excitedly seeks expansion.
Unto which unfathomable world
are you so surely stretching
your youthful green fingertips towards?

-15-

In one of my tears,
a banyan seed fell,
though I don't know how, nor why,
it had become lodged in my eye.
Indiscernible as sand
upon the palms of my hands,
you could almost doubt its existence.
I guarded it until warmth and rain arrived,
then let it freely fall,
between the cracked bricks of an abandoned wall.

It was resistant,
and I trust it survived,
though in a thousand years
I won't be there to tell you
if my hope in it was true.
But let us say,
that undisturbed,
in a crack of which no one knew,
roots furrowed into the ground,
red leaves uncurled,
and towards the sky,
branched fingers stretched out and grew.
Centuries on,
and the bricks of an old world,
of an abandoned building's walls,
are crumbled stones
in the heart of a tree
whose living roots consumed them,
and beneath whose shade
people gladly loiter:

weaving thoughts,
some thinkers think,
some doubters doubt,
and some dreamers also dream.
A girl,
fresh-faced, a fallen fig in hand,
sits wondering
about the size of a banyan seed,
the size of a tree,
and the aching gap of a thousand years between.

As she sits thinking,
a tear slides from her eye,
and in it is an idea,
almost invisible,
yet potent,
just like a banyan seed.
She watches it for a moment, upon her fingertips,
then summoning courage,
lets it slip free,
and although she won't be around to know,
it really will grow,
just like the banyan tree.

-16-

My body has become a river of nectar:
in fact,
where is my body?
It is no longer here, nor there…

With a triumphant cry of joy,
it vanished into my mind.
And where is my mind?
The ocean has become utterly still,
its profoundest depths have risen
right up to surface,
and there is not even a ripple.

The hand that reaches out to disturb that surface
stops, unable,
faced with
perfect stillness,
and upon that mirror,
the distilled essence
of ecstasy.

-17-

Don't you know
that God is not a philosophy?
Haven't you felt
infinity weaving its way
in and out of this world
in the scent of orange-blossoms
upon the spring breeze?
Hasn't you heart
ever been stirred
by the ecstatic call
of azahar hanging upon the air,
by the aroma of those waxy-white flowers
that bloom only for the short portion of a season,
then fall?

-18-

Stillness is not cessation,
it is a continuous flow;

stillness is not a dried-up river,
it is a ceaseless current;

stillness is rain falling in such torrents
that there is is no space between the raindrops,
only an endless cascade, pouring;

water moving
uninterrupted;

mind flowing
interminably;

stillness is not emptiness,
nor the annihilation of emotion;
it is the mind held unbroken
in an ecstatic stream,
with no pause
for anything else between.

-19-

The mind longs for the essence of the mind,
longing yearns for the essence of longing,
the body's cells,
desiring to comprehend the essence of desire,
impel the imagination
to seek the source of imagining.
Love seeks the essence of love,
and its search, until realised, is not unconditional:
it demands an answer.
Life, incessantly,
goes on searching for the essence of itself.

-20-

The Goddess of Wisdom came to drink
from the waters of sorrow.
She drank deeply and long,
and as she drank the river sang a song
which none could decipher.
They knew not if its verses spoke of sadness or of felicity.

The draught that she took seemed unending,
so great that day was her thirst for sorrow.
The winds came to watch her drinking,
joining the water's murmuring,
wondering all the while
how that water must burn inside her.
And so it did,
yet she did not stop drinking, the Goddess of Wisdom.

The stars, entering with the dusk,
were awed to witness her courageous feat,
though if it had not been her
they would have named it folly,
for who could bear such sorrow inside them,
they rightly pondered,
and were at a loss to what its end could be.
With the arrival of dawn they wondered
if indeed there would be an ending.

Yet,
there was, and with the glint of the morn
she lifted her lips from her burning draught,
face to the sun,
and the river changed its song, rejoicing,

the wind changed its tune, rejoicing,
the stars, already almost faded, rejoiced,
and the sun blessed the world in gold.

Now all understood the meaning of the Goddess's thirst:
wisdom had drunk from the water of sorrow
and transformed it into joy.

-21-

She who has never stuck our her tongue
to capture raindrops dripping
from a passion-flower's shamelessly ostentatious petals,
who has never broken that fruit's bitter skin
with her teeth,
sucked out its acid juice,
and wiped her lips with left-over dew,
although her stomach may be full,
she is also hungry.

She is also hungry
who has never tasted the horizon
upon the leaves of wet mint,
roamed barefoot upon the pasture with cows,
dried herself in post-rain-shower sun,
her soul eating the last remnants of the clouds.
No matter what else she has eaten,
she is also hungry.

She who has never consumed apples
less than perfect, far too sour,
manoeuvring around the wormholes,
crushing the scent of fermenting fallen fruit
beneath her feet,
is so hungry
that she has become numb to hunger.

Chomping on plastic,
on packets labelled under the misnomer of food,
slurping pre-prepared feelings from syrups of happiness,
digesting normality

with the assistance of doctor's prescriptions for heartburn,
doesn't she know that she is famished?

Doesn't she know
that kicking off those toe-pinching shoes,
those stockings steeping her feet in their own sweat,
skin submerged too long in the marshlands of confusion,
those heels that sink into the mud
as soon as you try to walk off the path onto wet grass,
that kicking off those shoes,
daring to taste the lilac-coloured petals of wild chicory,
surprised that they are not poison,
would cure her anaesthetised hunger?

Isn't there a doctor
who will tell her
that hunger can be remedied by the smell of earth,
of rain,
and by shrieking in horror
after accidentally eating a worm
in one of those over-sour apples
plucked with her own hands?
Or does such a prescription
carry too many uncertain side-effects?

-22-

'You are to be a bridge-maker,'
my dreams they spoke to me and said,
'but seek not for hammers or for stones
with which to build:
your bridges will be for those
who have grown old and weary of this world,
for those who were lost when young,
their dreams forgotten or spoiled,
those for whom the world seems only painful,
and those who seek a gleam of joy
but know not where to look.

Your bridges will not cross over freeways,
surpass rivers or trickling singing streams,
cross roads, paths nor mountain passes:
they will be bridges from one heart to another,
they are bridges of dreams.

Bridges for those who are lonely
and for those who weep,
bridges for those who lie in slumber and in sleep,
bridges for those who were born today,
and for those who are dying,
bridges for those who ask why,
and for those who don't ask,
bridges for those who've lost their way
amidst the cold and the dark.

Your bridges will pass over walls,
and walls will crumble beneath them,
awaken will those who are sleeping,

smile will those who are dying,
weep will those who sought joy,
and dry their eyes will those who were crying.

'You are to be a bridge-maker,'
my dreams they spoke to me and said,
'building bridges of love
between one human heart and another,
bridges of joy and wonder
built with courage and laughter,
bridges to crumble down walls
and connect each one of us with each other.'

-23-

We are breathing each other's air
all the time,
one life passes to another,
pulsates with the other.

You breath out
as the trees breath in.
The grass and leaves breath in, then out.

As you breath
the dark-daybreak stars
weave their way into you,
along with the mountains.

The sky is as near as the earth
which inhales between your toes,
as the mountains in your lungs,
as the cold silence
which prompts blood to tingle warm
in your fingers,
throbbing and mingling with the breath of morning.

Where are the spaces you had perceived?
The well conversed gap
between you and the universe?
Your body is the breath
of an interwoven rotation
of planets and stars
as you kneel in a wordless worship
which asks for nothing,
only to breath and breath,

earth watered with tears
which are also drops on leaves of trees.

Your breath and that of the dawn
weave around each other in rapturous wonder,
blood circulating
with the earth's rotations.
The earth between your toes is also alive,
the morning breaths in and out
with the universe
and your breath is lost
somewhere there.

-24-

A giant engine
churns out potions of cynicism
and we consume one grey concoction
after the other
to counter the effects of the last.

Instead of citizens
we produce cynics,
ardent believers in non-belief,
converted to the religion of hedonistic meaninglessness.
Love is reconstructed
as a manipulative game,
humility as foolishness
and sacrifice as futility.

Leave these streets for a moment:
just for a moment be reckless enough
to abandon their factories of narcissistic emptiness.

Be brave enough
to enter a garden,
go and look at a flower
and watch it bloom.
Fill yourself with a flower's unexplainable desire
to open and unfold.
Ponder a moment its innate need to grow.
Offer the water you were about to drink,
allow yourself to be thirsty,
and take pleasure in your thirst.

When you leave the garden,

protect yourself with the vision of a flower blossoming
again and again in your mind.

When others offer mocking laughter,
just smile,
and point them to the garden.
Tell them to watch a flower bloom,
over and over,
until their cynicism becomes painful,
until doubt becomes wonder,
wonder love,
and love sacrifice.
Until they offer the water they were going to drink,
and that offering, though no one sees it,
has significance.

-25-

A bowed head,
subdued voice,
unassuming disposition,
are not my choice
as symbols of humility.

My humility
is a flawless shining sword,
sharpened,
which moves not to any whims of mine
but to my principles.

Humility is in wielding it
with firmly planted feet,
unshielded but for a
head high-held, eyes straight,
desire-less:

obeying its command
despite knowing you will accuse me,
defame me,
blame and abuse me.

My hands are fixed
un-tilting
to my blade's hilt.
Its weight is my humility:
its force and power
bow me down
to integrity,
honesty

and dignity.

These are the only alters
upon which I offer my sword,
in return for a firmer voice,
a stronger stride,
and clear unfaltering eyes
which do not shy-down,
nor hide.

-26-

What are you waiting for?
the swing is at its zenith,
and your outstretched legs have reached their limit
as long as your hands keep clasping to the chains.
Jump!

Your barefoot-toes are touching
the sun at its meridian,
the tickling of air on uncovered skin
is calling,
and your untied hair
has already entangled itself with the wind.
Jump!

If you don't let go,
your only option is descent,
together with the swing,
its solid seat and chains.
You have reached the radius
of their jurisdiction.

You have only a split-second to decide:
Jump!

Your mind has wings:
carried by the cry for freedom,
upon the momentum of utter abandon,
they will unfurl and fly away.

-27-

A seed sprouts in the earth,
a seed sprouts in my mind,
the first seed sprouts at the beginnings of time:
is it the same seed sprouting
over and over?

Joy sprouts from a seed,
the ecstatic birth of the world
replicating itself,
again and again.

To experience the exhilaration
of opening up and growing,
divinity is born in innumerable nondescript forms,
and the earth nourishes uncountable seeds,
giving birth continuously.

For that same sprouting of joy
in the womb of the self,
this one worthless wanderer
stepped out from her door, unthinking,
and began walking through the rain,
the rapturous beginnings of time
recreating themselves all over again
within her awakening heart.

-28-

You tell me that I'm crazy,
perhaps just a little,
maybe substantially,
but let me also ask you,
with a playful gleam in the corner of my eyes,
if you can tell me honestly,
that you are really happy?

You tell me that I'm somewhat mad,
and I allow you to tell me,
but let me also ask you
if you can look me in the eyes
and tell me that what I'm doing is not working?

Tell me again,
about my lunacy,
that orange is too bright a colour,
that ideals have their limits,
that a light dose of cynicism is healthy,
but then let me ask you,
who is the one smiling here?

I think that maybe you are trying to convince yourself,
not me,
but that you haven't even quite managed that.
I think that maybe
you are scared of the unalloyed love
and natural innocence
inside you that is calling,
that you are frightened and attracted both at once.

I'll let you tell me that I'm mad,
but then allow me to extend an invitation
to come join me,
for it is a blissful madness
born from simple purity
and pure love.
Why not discard your fears a moment
and come to dance and bathe in it?

-29-

I am a calabash flask, sealed,
and inside,
I am full of expanding light:
light which battles against me
and longs to break out into the stars.
There is a fight going on:
am I the calabash,
or am I the furious radiance
that seeks to shatter me?

I am the husk of a calabash,
dried and painted,
polished and perforated
so that a flame shines through me:
I am the shell, I am the light,
and sometimes too,
I am the objects I illuminate,
and the flickering dance of the shadows
that romance around them.

I am a calabash gourd,
tender, green,
dangling between curling tendrils
and drooping leaves.
I am desire-less:
pluck and eat me,
I pine not for my skin to harden around me
and fix its form.

A calabash is nothing:
it is a container,

born to filled,
and moulded, and broken,
to carry water, light, and air.

-30-

Watery currents of sadness
mingle with hope and streams of anguish,
entwined with pure gladness,
lap upon my boat's hull:
escape their touch I shall not,
feel them I surely shall.
Every boat is, finally, a hollowed shell.
The river only flows around its body,
while within remains a hallowed, silent space.
Even if, perchance,
stormy waves deliver themselves
into that consecrated place,
again I shall remove them,
and again there shall be peace,
even as sorrow at times caresses
and at times dashes
against my battered hull.

-31-

A dark morning,
and no one,
except for the sound of rain,
falling upon the trembling earth.
I had not been waiting,
but nonetheless,
she came,
and I sit listening,
to her pitter-pattering,
as all sleep
except for the rain and I.
Without whispers even,
we share this secret meeting
of earth and sky
replenishing each other.

-32-

Haven't you felt it,
that beauty, pouring and pouring into you?
It can neither be expressed,
nor restrained.

Water keeps on flowing
into the terracotta pot,
despite its walls.
Where should it go?
How long can it be contained?

Perhaps the only way
is to throw the pot into the ocean,
water inside and out.

Clay, you know,
is only earth and water,
dehydrated.

Now it will absorb the water again,
become itself again.

-33-

If you have not drunk for a day,
oh, that is but a little thirst.
Wait another day,
and another.
Wait through the play of a life-time,
and as long as the life-cycle of a cosmos.

When you find the well,
you will be scared to drink:
the last taste you have had of water
was at the beginning of time,
when creation awoke
from sleeping consciousness
and spoke within living cells.

Pull the bucket from this well,
fill your flask up with infinity.
Start drinking slowly.
You wont be able to stop.
Thirst is when you wake up mad,
claimed by a dream
to feel water streaming
down your throat again.

-34-

I am happy sitting
outside the palace walls,
contemplating
long grass swaying
upon the evening sun.

As others gaze
upon luxurious constructions,
longing for things they have not,
I am devouring
the smell of rosemary and morning dew
upon my legs,
and the purple of jacaranda
painted upon the premonition of a storm.

Offer me a royal life,
and I shall refuse:

I know your queen
once loved to sleep beneath the stars,
outside between the earth and heaven,
so you built her
a mirrored-crystal room indoors,
and all were in awe of this wondrous imitation,
praising the king's abundant love.

I can only ponder
his strange cruelty,
mentally planning
a secret escape route from the palace,
through which I will aid the imprisoned queen

to flee in secret,
into my own castle of stars,
where we shall laugh,
and breath,
and be free.

-35-

Humble yourself a moment, great 'leader':
when will you realise that the treatises
of empathy and humanity are no malignant poison?
Kneel down, the earth digging into your knees,
and with reverence remember that without her
your feet would have no foundation to support them.
Bend and beg forgiveness
for adherence to the doctrine of conquest
and betrayal of your Mother.

How many times,
as the avatar of destruction,
must you appear brazenly
displaying the epithet of 'saviour',
in a few impertinent strokes
slaying languages, people, wisdom,
because they are humbler than your own,
squeezing blood from the veins
of those less arrogant
but more human than yourself?

Humble yourself a moment,
long enough to gaze at the pathway
of conquest left behind you:
it is empty of victories,
bestrewn with ruins.
You have conquered no one,
not even your self.

How long will you keep building palaces
upon heaps of wreckage?

Why not try an open field, just once.
Just once, create a new foundation.
Then, perhaps, your dynamism,
mingled with the water of humility,
might become a consecration to the earth.

-36-

There is a lane
decorated with sweet smiles,
sickly sweet
like a road full of fallen mangoes
rotting in the sun,
crawling with worms;

decorated with carelessness,
the downward path of a bicycle,
fast and easy,
except that the wind is not fresh,
it is made of webs of sticky sugar
filled with tiny biting flies
which entrap
and consume you;

made from embraces of deceit,
fed with delusions of love,
empathy-less,
caresses of viscous candy
chewed and dribbled
from a desiring mouth,
mixed with salt on sweaty skin,
aroma-less flowers
filled with chemical perfumes
which close around you,
and there you are,
drunkenly enjoying a swim
in a barrel of corrosive acid
as it eats you.

On the horizon there is sunlight
upon the expanse of the river,
a cool breeze among the leaves,
the first scatterings of afternoon rain,
a bird's call,
a child's laughter.
Hope and sadness mingle
in a strange melancholy upon the wind.

-37-

Even in the streets of millionaires
there are oxidised fences with peeling paint,
there are dry fallen leaves,
mosquitoes,
there is an owl run over by a car
on the side of the pavement,
its yellow eyes glinting no more.

Even in the streets of millionaires,
there exists attachment,
unanswered questions,
life coming and going,
abandoned swimming pools growing slime,
and lonely houses.

Even in the streets of millionaires
there are whispers of the meaning of life,
and it is beautiful,
as beautiful as patterns of rust on metal,
as a bird's twig-nest inside the garden of a mansion,
as lichen growing on a decaying tree trunk.

-38-

Strangely, I stirred in the night,
though it seemed to me day,
for I did not feel darkness,
nor was I dreaming.

My body was a field
upon which glinting sun and dew
with the earth had spoken,
and so many seeds of happiness
had yielded forth a meadow of poppies,
crumpled petals swaying
in a guise of daintiness,
playing with the wind.
They are wild-flowers,
endemic and impossible to uproot,
you cannot destine when they'll bloom,
but the shoots of their million seeds
are always present, hiding,
and their crumpled petals are not an ephemeral fraud,
they are everlasting.

In the night,
with the song of a thousand poppies dancing
upon my body
from seeds so long in waiting,
I awoke.

-39-

For whom do I wait,
at the open door of night,
between the darkness of an unlit house
on one side,
and the new-moon sky
on the other?
None will cross the shore of solitude
into my silent home this midnight hour,

and yet I wait.

I have promised myself to no one,
my only appointment
is with the moody clouds
and the shadowless whispers of trees,

and yet I wait,
expectantly,

for a visitor
who fixes no time of arrival,
whose only footsteps
are the beats of my palpitating heart,
and whose lamp leads straight
to the inner rooms
of my little house,
filling it with waves
of ecstasy.

We have met before,
somewhere,

some other night,
in secret,

and although I don't remember
any promise of return,

I wait,
and keep on waiting,
because the dark sky
whispers
that You will come again.

-40-

Some tremble with fear,
others
with aversion or despair.

My heart beats with none of these,
but with a joy unsurpassable.
Am I afraid?
And of what?
That I cannot contain this flow of bliss inside me?
Or that I am imperfect
and the responsibility of expressing such a gift
not only in action but in every thought,
is overwhelming?

It is not an offer to receive timidly
yet nor does it come with possibility of refusal,
and so with trembling hands, I accept.

-41-

The whole universe poured in and out of me one day.
I grew as old and as young
as the beginning of time,
as innocent and as wise.

After that I wandered long,
wondering who I was,
whether these hands and feet,
feelings and thoughts,
were mine or were not.
What I found is that which is mine, is not,
that which is not, is,
and that the answer to paradoxes
lies in the paradox.

So I let it be.
Old and young,
soft and hard,
foolish and sagacious all at once:
the universe reveals the truth of itself
expressed through insignificance.

-42-

Tonight I will curl up to sleep
upon the lap of this red earth.
Purple crocuses of saffron will bloom around me,
and I will dream so many dreams,
benevolent ones, because my mother is so,
and the stars will be a blanket upon my skin:
they are warm, not cold, you know,
and they also sing,
the melodies of harp strings plucked by light.

In this web of dreams I will lie,
and in the morning I shall see
that in my sleep I was weeping,
and my tears became dew on the grass.
One part of them will nourish the roots of life,
the other will ascend to the clouds.
They are tears neither of sorrow,
nor of joy,
they are something else.

Yes, tonight I will sleep
in the terracotta lap of my mother earth,
and when I awake,
something will have changed:
she will have become a part of me.

-43-

How pure your heart,
how pure it is.
Don't tell me otherwise:
without your permission,
I have already seen it.

On top of it are so many things constructed,
simply for the sake of living,
strange labyrinths made from denial,
with dead ends built from rejection,
layers of wrapping paper
messily tied in tangled, knotted ribbons.
Let's unwrap them…

Inside is a gift:
your heart, so perfectly pure,
so authentic you've kept it,
even while wrapped up in angst.
Don't worry, I won't hurt it.
Let's untie those tangled ribbons,
unwrap the bound up miracle within.

-44-

One night I went out into the dark,
unwrapped the clothes of shame and shyness,
and sitting in a silent place
collected together sadness,
failure, fear,
and humiliation's taunting mockery,
mingled jointly with complicity.

Under the aphotic new-moon sky
I called a reunion
with torturous desires seeking unconditional replies
not to be found within this world:
love, comprehension, rest and relief.

In the company of shadows
darker than the moonless sky I sat,
and did not talk,
I only watched them, waiting,
until some power on the eerie breeze
whispered strangely of a smile.

Inviting them inside me
at a focused point,
I moved them upwards within me,
and such a liberating force I felt,
as each became not what it appeared to be
but what it really was,
pain seeking the essence of its own desires,
piercing through the layers of itself.

With a violent joyful tremor,
my self leaped beyond itself,
the obscured moon was revealed,
sadness looked at me strangely, cried out,
tore off her sombre veil,
and was so bright I hardly dared to see.
Fingertips of fear, caressing completion,
dissolved,
and life's longings, agonisingly unfulfilled
gazed upon me,
revealing themselves as the eyes of the Beloved:

in my body, a tremulous, wild joy,
and then silence, not even a breath…

Returning I could only say:
'it is true, it is true,
all hopes and promises,
they are true, they are all true!'

If still I love the moonless night
and go there to embrace and delight in the darkness,
it is because to me she has unmasked herself as joy,
irresistible,
moving triumphantly inside me.

Because of her I came back whispering:
'it is real, it is real,
every exultation ever promise will be fulfilled.'

-45-

Alone,
in front of the fire,
flickering flames consuming what were trees,
I sat and watched my dreams:

you were weeping
and reaching over, I wiped your tears
with the sleeve-end of my shirt,
soft overused cotton,
good only for comfort, not for appearances.

Watching myself in the flames,
I did not tell you 'do not cry.'

Your tears are in the fabric of my clothes now.
What shall I do with them?
They have become a part of me
and cannot be washed out.

No, I did not tell you 'do not cry.'
I told you 'smile a little, between the tears.
Don't you know that in sadness
tears fall from the inside of the eyes,
in joy from the outside?'

Smile a little, and we will see if both can fall at once.
That is hope.
Smile a little,
and we will see if one can transform into the other.
If I shall have your tears dampen my clothes,
then let them at least be of both kinds.

So you smiled,
and watching myself in the flames,
it is I who began to cry.
I don't know how the fire kept on burning,
with so many tears falling into it.

-46-

Receding for a while into the cave of my heart,
I sat and thought.

The words that arose there,
spoken from silent depths,
told me:
'to love without desire of return
is an act of great courage.
From that valiant act,
a great tranquillity will flow into a fill you,
a deep peace.
Your motives shall be only what they are,
with no secondary ones,
and your mind, free of deceit,
will know the strength of self-possessed calm,
imperturbable.'

Having felt the truth of that serenity upon me,
I took courage as told,
and stepped from the cave of my heart
into the world.

-47-

Unexpectedly,
I found myself sleeping
in a land with no walls,
no windows barred,
beyond even thirst
or desire,
there was no torment of the space
between me and freedom.
I slept not in the depths of dream,
but in the depths of all that was real.

-48-

Intangible things
take flight
inside me.

Colourless colours.

Wordless words.

Hope.

Dreams.

Love
with an invisible orientation.

A caress without hands.

The essence of a smile.

Intangible things
fly in and out of my mind
from uncharted lands,

set lose within,
ensuring
that nothing will ever be the same
again.

-49-

Sleeping,
the purring of a cat
mingled
with tears.

I dreamt of things
both sad
and beautiful.

Of a little tongue
licking salt from my cheeks,
licking away the conversations going on
outside my window
about what I had and had not done
to whom.

I dreamt that my heart,
instead of beating,
purred.

That those yellow eyes,
without over-simplifying things,
understood me,
hidden under everything else that wasn't.

I didn't mind
that it was only a cat.

-50-

How many stories can run in the river
of one person's veins?
The taste of how many different types of tears?
For she takes only the tears and the torments
and leaves the smiles for their owners.

Who is she,
the exorcist?
Does she also have a story?
And what does she become?
For she does not become the others,
though she carries a part of their pain.

Sometimes she thinks
that one day she will also share her tears and memories,
lay her head upon a gentle shoulder,
but she never does.
Her fate is already set
as the extractor of others' woes.

Who is she,
this exorcist?
She is the orange burning of fire,
which when her time is up
leaves only cold ashes.
Did she becomes the ashes?
No, that was the wood,
her collection of stories.
She was the flames.
She came and went,
took some tears and left some laughter,

took some sadness and left some hope.
Some blamed her for the pain of being freed
and others thanked her for their freedom.

Where go the flames when the fire is out?
What happens to her, and who is she,
the silent exorcist of sorrows?
Does she have a story of her own?
No one ever asked her,
and no one knows.

-51-

I have a repetitive dream
of myself dreaming
of a shoulder to lean my head upon and weep,
a shoulder made of the aroma of jasmine at night
and the purring of a cat;
there are hands made of moonlight,
soothing,
to wipe the salty drops of the sea
trickling down my cheeks.

These are my feelings,
I am not adorning them
only for sake of poetry.

It is not a dream of sadness,
nor surprise,
not even joy.
The only desire of my tears is to rest a moment,
to be understood and pardoned,
untangled
from a world of misunderstandings and expectations:
pardoned equally for their sins
and for their talents,
for their hopes, failures, and inconsistencies,
for their ordinariness
when they could have been greater
and their arrogance
when they should have been humble.

Where is that aromatic shoulder,
those moonlight-fingers

on my tear-wet face?
Where is my release,
my moment of relief?

On waking
I know that dreams are symbols of others things,
that there is no rest in this world.
Tears are intangible desires trying to take form,
salt dreaming of the ocean,
and feelings which end somewhere beyond themselves.

-52-

Upon a tightrope I walked,
on either side, nothing,
emptiness,
and things made of light and shadow,
temptations and taunting.

Below,
no, don't look below,
and don't fall!

Under my feet a tight drawn wire,
one foot carefully in front of the other.
Where am I going,
and how much longer is there?
Don't wobble,
no one will catch you!

And then,
I noticed something:
the wire was gone!

There was only air.
But I did not fall.
Such freedom!
I was flying!

-53-

There was a girl in the park,
her face a-swirl with tears
as she gazed at the last autumn leaves
drifting down
from almost naked branches.

Her tears
were the most beautiful thing I had seen:
that she had not fear to cry,
that she was alive!

The branches, bare,
had revealed themselves.
She too, was unafraid.
Yet all that passers-by would think
was that something was wrong,
that she was sad.

She was the autumn weeping,
the premonition of life at the end of things.
I watched but did not desire comfort her,
and I hoped that no one else would,
severing short her valiant reverie.

-54-

Something was wrong.
I could not place exactly what,
a strange dullness hovering around.
Something missing.

Then I understood:
my child was not laughing.

Sometimes when she was sad she would cry.
But now there was only silence,
strange and grey.

My child was missing!

The clouds had no form,
only an amorphous mass of whiteness,
the leaves did not laugh,
the rain had no rhythm,
the trees no feelings.
I could have uprooted every seedling
then and there
and they would not have cried.

I did not care about the scientific
or mystic
explanations of rainbows,
the passion-fruit's seeds were offensive,
and I couldn't imagine a thousand capricious vines
growing from them any more.

The birds woke me in the morning

with their noise,
and the children playing where also noisy,
nothing more.

My child was missing!

The snow was cold and unpleasant,
the wind was a nuisance,
the stars had no secrets.

How had I not noticed?
How many days had I neglected her,
alone without play?
Where had I left her?
Had she run away?
Was she still alive?

Frantically I wondered how to find her.
I heard a whimpering.
With my worry she had awoken,
but she was weak,
I had left her sleeping suffocated
under a pillow of trivialities.

In my arms I held her
and we fed each other
with imaginations of scientific experiments
carried out just for fun,
classifications of the different types of river currents
gleaned through observations
of leaf-boats racing each other;
we fed each other
by planting watermelon seeds in the garden

and waiting impatiently,
celebrating when they grew;
we fed each other with absurdity and meaning,
stupidity and profundity,
laughter cloaked with secret silent glances.

We slept together in a hammock
under stars in the breeze,
told stories into the night.
And when the birds woke us in the morning
it was with singing,
not just noise.

-55-

Don't resist happiness:
cast off the layers of clothes
you have carried all your life,
and run,
run with the breeze of delight upon your skin,
whatever be the season,
through snow or flowers,
ice as well as sun can fill you equally with life.

Cast aside your layers and layers of clothes
and run,
just run.
You are allowed to be happy,
no one is watching,
and even if they are,
who cares?

Even if you accidentally collide with someone
for lack of looking ahead,
and they see you like that,
unmasked,
Who cares?
Just smile,
spin in circles like a dervish,
dance,
give yourself permission to be free.

-56-

Immersed in the rushing river,
water flowing through my yielding body
as it lay there,
casting away debris and pebbles in its way,
washing away thither
the detritus and dregs
that clinging unseen hang to the corners of being:
'Flow, and flow through me,'
I urged the current on,
'until I am hollow inside,
until I'm transparent,
until there is no sadness,
no renting pain,
only light sparkling on water,
until you have washed away everything
except the sunlight, glittering.'

-57-

I consumed the bitter flowers of life,
crimson oleander petals full of poison,
but I did not die!
Who was it that drew this poison from my blood
and wove it into a garland of victory,
deep red,
to hang upon my door?

Who was it that took and transformed me
into a tiny embryo of life
wrapped in the hands of the cosmos,
wrapped in the hands of love?

As weightless as the wings of a butterfly
drinking dawn from dewdrops,
as the sun reflected in prisms
upon the wings of a dragonfly,
as a bird singing in the rain,
such has my life become.

Give me your open palms a moment:
the only thing left to make me happier
is to pour my happiness into those hands,
to see you smiling
full of luminescence and tears.

-58-

Oh world,
do with me as you please,
but you cannot remove the infinite sky
from this insignificant heart of mine!

Do with me as you please:
I have already drunk the sky
at dawn,
midday,
and at night,
crimson,
blue
and black-glittering.

I have already loved her
until she became part of me.

What is in my heart shall there remain,
though you may try to do with me as you like!

-59-

The touch of the ocean on bare skin,
salty collisions with waves,
the sea, expanding everywhere,
cannot be known only by watching.

Imagining serves to build curiosity
but does not fulfil thirst.
One day,
you will have to dive in.

Salt will sting your eyes,
you will swallow a little water,
and then you will swim.

Later, if you try leave the salt-water behind,
memories of saline caresses on skin,
of gulls calling
as you float between ocean and sky
wondering which side of infinity to sink into,
will keep on pulling you:
once you have known the sea,
there remains no chance of permanent departure.

-60-

Midnight:
stirring to the sound of rain falling.

Searching for miracles
in magic and spectacles,
you miss the marvel
moving inside you.

Peace, unasked for,
fills me,
an inward smile,
no one watching,
as rain falls to a silent audience of one.

Why should I search
for any other kind of magic?

-61-

A new-moon night:

tonight without shame we shall meet,
not even the memory of cloth
between us,
myself and the dark,
myself, the earth, and the Formless One.

Tonight without shame,
love,
fearlessly,
shall move inside me.

You have not known the meaning of ecstasy
until you have risked love directly
with the Unknown One,
not any human form
between your skin and the dark,
between your heart,
the intimacy of the infinite,
and the night.

-62-

One joy once known
transforms into another,
even as I hardly ask.

Body still,
the heart trembles,
then body trembling,
the heart is still,
and I don't know which is more marvellous
until I breath out
and in that serenity desire not
to breath in again.

In that stillness,
I am
and am not.

When finally,
painfully, I breath,
where I lie I move not
except for strange spasms of joy
quivering up inside me.

-63-

How many hues has joy?
What I thought could not be more
is ever more.

My fingers, trembling, touch eternity,
like the horizon caressing the sky,
wondering if it should become
that which it loves so much.
If I put my hand inside,
what will happen?
Will it disappear?
I would not have lost anything,
even then.
And what would it return as,
after that?
Will I even recognise my own fingers,
after that?

-64-

I fell in love with a tree one day,
curled up in the hollow carob's trunk,
wood winding around itself
like churning waves solidified.

At its feet lay a stone with a heartbeat,
and wrapping it in my arms
I lay there, enamoured with a carob tree
amidst a sea of laterite soil.

As the stone's heartbeat pulsated with my own
I dreamt of roots
that extended into the centre of the earth,
within which moved the succession of centuries,
of mythology and history all intertwined in continuity.
Upon their sustenance,
drawn deep from gnarled and secret pathways
through the soil,
branches grew and leaves sprouted,
drinking sunlight and moonlight,
and through their nipples I imbibed
all the stars in the sky,
as from outstretched arms grew seeds
with whispers of the world to come.

Times gone and times to be
flowed through me,
mingling with the smell of carob,
of knurled wood on naked skin,
of the heartbeat of a stone embraced.

So impassioned with the tree I was,
that I lost myself,
knew not where was I.

Stirring to the sun's touch on bare toes,
dancing between leaves,
voiceless I walked and wound myself
around and around the tree,
caressing it with my fingertips,
totally mad,
with memories of the beginning and endings of time
moving all around inside me.

When still I could not speak,
I lay and rolled in the red earth,
breathing the spiky scent of rosemary,
dazed and filled with the feelings of a tree,
until slowly, slowly I awoke,
though it was long before I spoke again,
not wanting to break my sweet delirium.

-65-

Yes, I have also fallen in love.
It just happened to me one day,
and kept on happening ever since.

Some days I am in love with smiles,
other days with tears;
in spring it is with the scent of azahar upon the breeze,
the aroma of a thousand waxy citrus blossoms;
in autumn it's a fascination
with the orange of persimmons,
globes of joy on naked branches;
I am in love with dew on rosemary
and with the sound of laughter mixed with birdsong.

In the morning the dawn kisses my eyes,
and in the evening that same sun wraps me to sleep.
I have lain in a river
in love with the caress of flowing water,
and alone in the night enamoured with every star.

I am in love with the morning dew
that rolls from your eyes,
be it in sorrow or be it in joy,
be it upon your cheeks or upon those of another:
I am in love with the hidden hopes of every heart,
and knowing not whom to embrace first,
I embrace everyone with my silence.

Everyday, I find myself falling in love:
with trees,
with sunlight upon the wings of a bee,

with the aspirations of a flower,
with the heartbeat of the soil,
with the deep slow song of a mountain,
and with the salt of the sea.

I don't know if I can teach you this love,
but certainly I will try.

-66-

I have only one unfulfilled love,
to whom I desired to offer the stars
as they had also flowed in and out of me,
yet all I could give were whispers
and stolen glimpses;
into whose hands I longed to pour
every joy that had ever moved inside me,
even if I would be left with only sadness
and memories,
yet all I could give
was a parting embrace and my hope.

There is no fulfilment
without things first unfulfilled,
no completeness
without things first uncompleted.

Who is my beloved?
Anyone,
whoever is searching
with hope and pain inside.

www.ingramcontent.com/pod-product-compliance
Lightning Source LLC
Chambersburg PA
CBHW030302010526
44107CB00053B/1778